The Last Forbidden Kingdom

MUSTANG

Land of
TIBETAN
BUDDHISM

Foreword by His Holiness the Dalai Lama

Photographs by Vanessa Schuurbeque Boeye
Text by Clara Marullo

Produced by Concepts Publishing Inc.

Charles E. Tuttle Co., Inc.
Boston • Rutland, Vermont • Tokyo

The Last Forbidden Kingdom

MUSTANG
Land of
TIBETAN
BUDDHISM

For Darsang, Wangdu, and Sonam,
and the children of Mustang

First published in the United States in 1995 by Charles E. Tuttle Company, Inc.

of Rutland, Vermont and Tokyo, Japan, with editorial offices at

153 Milk Street, Boston, Massachusetts 02109-4809

First Edition

Library of Congress Cataloging-in-Publication Data

Marullo, Clara.
    The Last Forbidden Kingdom, Mustang : land of Tibetan Buddhism /
written by Clara Marullo : photographed by Vanessa Schuurbeque
Boeye. -- 1st ed.
        p.   cm.
    ISBN 0-8048-3061-4
    1. Mustang (Nepal) --Description and travel.   2. Buddhism--Nepal-
-Mustang   I. Boeye, Vanessa Schuurbeque.   II. Title.
    DS493.53.M39   1995
    954.96--dc20   95-18837
                                                                CIP

Printed and bound in Hong Kong

NASHOBA REGIONAL HIGH SCHOOL
MEDIA CENTER

Acknowledgments

We extend our warmest thanks to:
His Holiness the Dalai Lama, for his support and inspiration; Kamptruel Rinpoche, our spiritual guide to Mustang, his wife Yumla, and his attendant monks Lobsang Tenda and Tenzing Lahwang; Tenzing Geyche Tetong, private secretary to the Dalai Lama; Salden Kunga and the monks of Namgyal monastery in Dharamsala, India; King Jigme Palbar Bista, for his help and hospitality; Tsewang Bista, our guide and interpreter; Charles Ramble, anthropologist, and foremost authority on the Mustang region; his assistant, Nima Deshgen; Lisa Choegyal of Tiger Mountain, Nepal, who arranged and managed our treks; Markus Ruedigar at Lufthansa; Manjushrl Thapa and the Annapurna Conservation Area Project; Michel Peissel, whose writing captivated us; Myra Shackley of the Nottingham Business School, for her report on tourism in Mustang; Dr. Lobsang Dolma Kangkar and Gill Marais, for their work on Tibetan Medicine; Helena Norberg-Hodge, for her elucidation of Tibetan village culture; our translators Yangcchen Yeshe and Jamchoe; Jill Bobrow, Dana Jinkins, and Tara Hamilton of Concepts Publishing Inc.; Gary Chassman of Verve Editions; The Discovery Channel, Inc.; Felicity Nock and Jo Lal, for their tireless help in organizing the project; Glen Marullo, for his constructive comments on the manuscript; and finally special thanks to Tony Miller of Intrepid Films—without whom none of this would have happened.

Vanessa S. Boeye
and
Clara Marullo

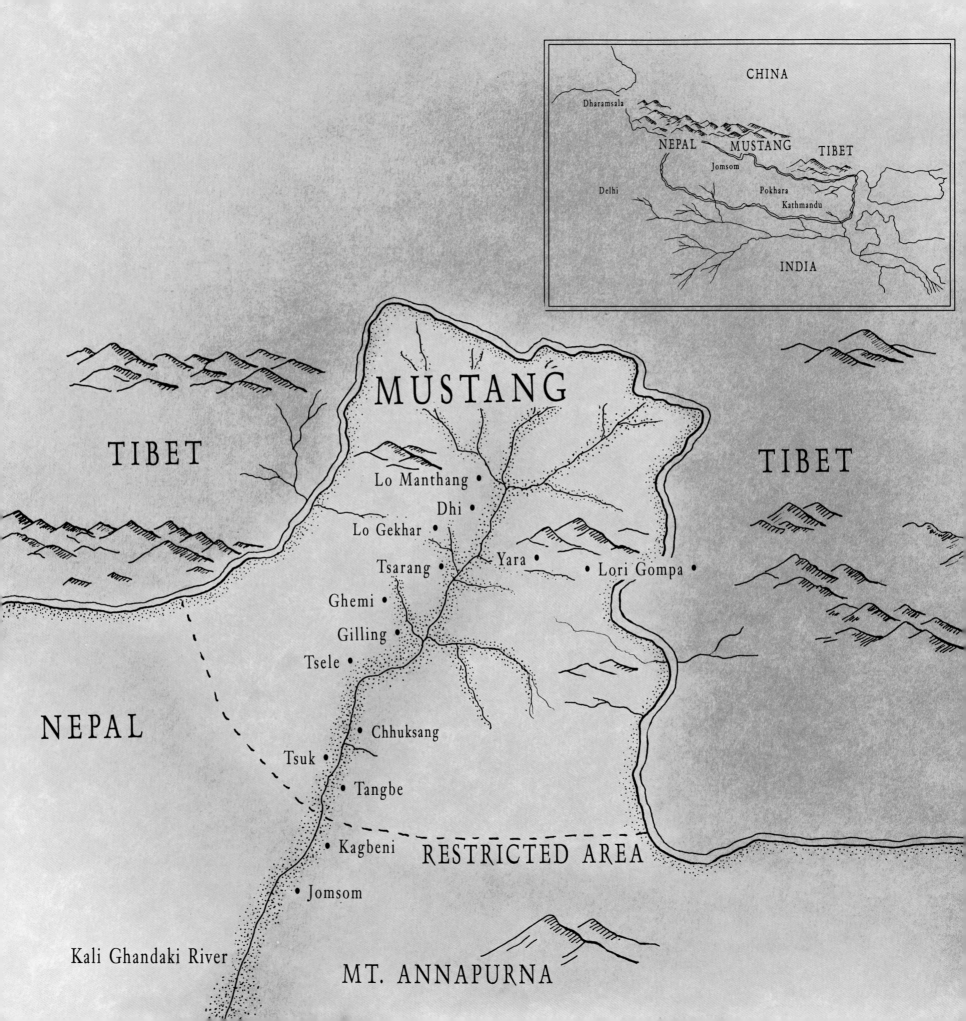

Contents

Foreword by His Holiness the Dalai Lama   2

1 The Land of Lo   6

2 Journey to Lo Manthang   24

3 King and Commoners   46

4 Rites of Passage   60

5 Making a Living   74

6 The Road to Nirvana   92

7 Conserving the Wilderness   114

Epilogue
Into the Future   126

Glossary   134

Foreword

Mustang is one of the few places in the Himalayan region that has been able to retain its traditional Tibetan culture unmolested. This pictorial book on Mustang explores a variety of Tibetan-related subjects. I am happy to learn that the main focus is the importance of maintaining the Tibetan culture. I strongly believe that Tibetan culture has the potential to make a positive contribution to today's world. It is, therefore, encouraging to see a growing interest in this subject.

Unfortunately, since the occupation of Tibet, Tibetan culture is facing the threat of extinction. The influx of Chinese immigrants to Tibet is marginalizing the Tibetans and their culture at an alarming pace. Our people are becoming an insignificant minority in their own land.

Today, because of hard work and dedicated efforts of the Tibetan refugee community, authentic Tibetan culture now survives only in exile and a few places like Mustang, which have had long historical and cultural ties with Tibet. I am confident that this book will not only help readers to learn about the uniqueness of Mustang but also will draw their attention and the need for support for the survival of the Tibetan people with their unique culture.

March 26, 1995   The Dalai Lama

Dawn. Gradually, the sun touches the bare-boned mountains, warming them to shades of ocher, and casting long shadows into the silence of the valley. As monks on the roof of a monastery blow long ceremonial horns, a lone figure emerges from the tiny walled city nearby. A man in his sixties, he walks solidly, with the confidence of one born to authority. He pauses briefly to turn the large prayer wheel next to the town gate, then sets off purposefully, circling the capital in the clockwise direction his faith has taught him, and muttering the mantras of his forefathers. Here and there he encounters peasants on their way to the fields. They greet him prayerfully, or touch their foreheads in a gesture of respect. For this is their king, Jigme Palbar Bista: and even now, as his long-forbidden kingdom hovers on the threshold of the modern world, he is the leader of a community where past and present, seen and unseen, still have indistinct boundaries.

I

The Land of Lo

Nestling like the missing piece of a jigsaw puzzle into the borders of western Tibet, the tiny kingdom of Mustang occupies 780 square miles in the upper valley of the Kali Ghandaki River, to the north of the main Himalayan massif. Strong winds, whipping up the chasm between Annapurna and Dhaulagiri, exacerbate an already extreme continental climate. These forces have fashioned a barren desert landscape, whose starkness is matched only by its grandeur. Survival in this harsh environment is difficult at best—even for the rugged people of the mountains. Fields must be hewn out of rubble, and precious water diverted for irrigation. Drought and altitude allow only one crop per year: failure can have severe consequences.

Despite these rigors, the "Land of Lo"—as it is known to its seven thousand inhabitants—developed a reputation for trade, and became in its

heyday a center of religious art and learning second only to Lhasa. Subsequent events though, made its isolation absolute. For most of the last thirty years, the kingdom has been sealed from the outside world for political reasons. The Chinese closed its northern border when they overran Tibet in the late 1950s. The Nepalese frontier to the south followed shortly afterward, when Mustang became the nerve center of a guerrilla war against the Chinese in occupied Tibet. Mustang remained off limits to outsiders until a massive popular uprising in Kathmandu at last introduced parlimentary democracy to Nepal in 1991. At this time, all previously restricted areas were partially reopened, and the first foreigners since French author Michel Peissel—who was granted a one-time permit in 1964—were able to make the arduous journey to Lo.

What westerners find is an anachronism: a tiny feudal kingdom scarcely changed since the Middle Ages—and one of the last centers of Tibetan culture not to have been radically altered by outside influences. Despite ever more pervasive pressure from Kathmandu to take shelter under the cultural umbrella of Nepal's Hindu majority, Mustang still remains staunchly Buddhist; its people retaining their Tibetan identity and customs.

First mentioned in Tibetan and Ladakhi chronicles as early as the seventh century, the Land of Lo seems to have become a principality within the the influence of Lhasa as a result of land granted to retainers of the Gungthang kings of western Tibet. As in Tibet, the population practiced the Bon faith indigenous to the region. Mustang's conversion to Buddhism was concurrent with that of the motherland. Some of the old animist ways were abandoned, but others were simply assimilated into the new religion. The most important of the early Tibetan sages and reformers were

Page 3: The Buddha Maitreya at Champa Lakhang
Pages 4&5: Mist enshrouds a stupa outside of Gilling.
Page 6: A charm used to ward off evil spirits
Page 7: The extraordinary cave monastery of Lori
Above: A Buddhist monk makes an offering of incense.
Right: A gilt statue of Maitreya adorned with white khatas in Champa Lakhang
Page 9: Monks on the roof of Namgyal Monastery (north of Lo Manthang) summon the faithful to prayer with long ceremonial horns.

also active in Lo—most notably the great founder of Tibetan Buddhism, Padmasambhava. It is said that his completion of Samye (Tibet's oldest monastery) was dependent on the building of the temple of Lo Gekhar in eastern Mustang.

Little is known of early potentates, but by the late 1300s one crucial figure emerges: a warrior named Ame Pal. Regarded as the father of today's royal lineage, he subdued local warlords to unite the kingdom, governing his conquests from the great fortress of Ketchen Dzong. As his rule became consolidated, Ame Pal constructed a capital in its shadow. Known as Lo Manthang, after "the plain of aspiration" on which it stands, the city subsequently gave its name to the kingdom: Mustang is a cartographer's corruption of Manthang.

A devout Buddhist, Ame Pal then built monasteries and temples, and persuaded the renowned Sakya lama and teacher, Ngorchen Kunga Sangpo, to come from Tibet to consecrate them. The great man hesitated for seven years, until he saw an auspicious sign in the sky. At last, in 1427, he embarked on the first of three historic visits to Lo, returning in 1436 and 1447. Later, he developed a special relationship with Mustang, initiating a religious revival, and establishing a chain of monasteries. The lama's legacy is everywhere—from the predominance of the Sakya sect (during the Mongol period, Lo became its western stronghold) to the wealth of art and sacred texts commissioned under his influence. As a result, the kingdom grew rapidly during the fifteenth and sixteenth centuries, to become one of the most important centers of religious activity in the Tibetan world.

Pages 10 & 11: The medieval walled city of Lo Manthang
Above: King Jigme Palbar Bista and reincarnate lama Kamptruel
Rinpoche spin prayer wheels.
Page 13: Monks approach the stupa that forms the gateway
to Tsarang.

Page 14: Monks make an offering at the shrine at Drakhmar.
Above: View from a distance of the caves at Drakhmar

Secular pressures were never absent though. Ame Pal's capital was fortified with walls twenty feet high. It was provided with only one great gate, which is still closed at dusk, as it was in medieval times. The city was to withstand repeated wars, initially involving local bandits, and later with the kingdom of Jumla, on its southwestern frontier. Today an undistinguished village at the foot of the Dhaulagiri range, Hindu Jumla was for more than four centuries Mustang's most powerful political rival. Although separated by the highlands of Dolpo, conflict between the two states see-sawed until the eighteenth century. Peaceful interludes saw great expansion and the construction of castle-towns such as Tsarang and Ghemi.

Religious life continued to thrive. As both Lo and Dolpo were regarded as outlying provinces of Tibet, cultural interchange abounded. Lamas from Dolpo traveled to Tibet using the more accessible route through Lo Manthang. The monks of Mustang frequently went to the motherland for instruction. In addition, Lo itself became a place of pilgrimage renowned throughout the Himalayan region.

Mustang also stood at the heart of a commercial empire that stretched from Tibet down into India. The relative ease with which men and beasts can cross the passes on the kingdom's northern border (most are under fifteen thousand feet), combined with good access through the Kali Ghandaki Valley, meant that Mustang occupied a strategic position. It was not the most important point along the route, but its control

Pages 16 & 17: The valley between Tsarang and Lo Manthang
Above: Spinning wool is a pastime of the elderly.
Page 19: Sheep and goats are reared for markets in Pokhara and the Kathmandu Valley.
Detail: The dzo, a rugged yak/cow crossbreed, adapts well to Mustang's harsh conditions.

of the border passes made Mustang a crucial player—particularly in the salt trade from Tibet. The system involved many middlemen. In a land where agriculture is unreliable, trade provided the people of Lo with a vital source of alternative income.

Essentially, it was a simple process of barter. Tibetan salt, from distant lakes north of the Tsangpo River, was exchanged for wheat, barley, and rice grown in the fertile valleys of Pokhara and Kathmandu. Traders from Mustang and Dolpo would travel with yak, *dzo* (a yak/cow crossbreed), pack goats, and even sheep carrying grain to centers on the Tibetan frontier. Here it would be exchanged for salt, which in turn was carried down to villages such as Tukche in the Kali Ghandaki Valley. It could then either be stored until growers from the south arrived with their harvest, or sold on to Thakali merchants to be transported further down the line. Although salt formed the backbone of the business, there was also a thriving trade in livestock, wool, and all kinds of foodstuffs along this axis.

Small wonder that the kings of Jumla made such persistent attempts to gain control of the region. Although Mustang had become a protectorate of Ladakh at the end of the sixteenth century, Jumla's rulers remained undeterred. Such was their persistence that they even tried to ransom the Lo-pa queen. In 1719, the king of Mustang had arranged to marry a Ladakhi princess, but on her way to Lo Manthang for the wedding she was captured by Jumlan bandits and imprisoned at Kagbeni. Although her husband sent his finest warriors to free her, their efforts failed, and she was forced to remain incarcerated for many months, until troops from Ladakh and Parbat came to her rescue.

Around 1740, Jumla again attacked—and won, as Ladakh had lost its former power, and could no longer offer assistance. It was to be a glorious but short-lived conquest. Just forty years later, Jumla itself was obliterated by Prithvi

Narayan Shah—the first of the great Gorkha kings who unified Nepal. Despite its strategic position, Mustang was largely ignored by the Gorkhas. The treaty of 1802, which demanded annual tribute in exchange for protection, allowed the kingdom to retain a large measure of autonomy.

The reemergence of the Shah dynasty in the 1950s however, and the partial democratization of Nepal that followed, stripped the king of much of his power. China's invasion of Tibet then forced Mustang into the resistance movement. The kingdom became home to some six thousand warriors from eastern Tibet. Known as the Khampas, these tall, handsome men fought a bitter war along Mustang's northern border.

Although their campaign was virtually unreported in the West, the Khampas were secretly financed by the CIA. Many of their leaders were air-lifted to Camp Hale in Colorado, and returned to Mustang trained for guerrilla warfare. Equipped only with an outdated collection of swords and rifles, the Khampas nonetheless achieved significant results. They managed to recapture parts of southern and eastern Tibet, gather vital intelligence, and greatly damage Chinese communications.

Despite local sympathy for their cause, the Khampas' continued presence in Mustang caused great hardship for the Lo-pas, placing an insupportable burden both on their resources, and their relationship with Kathmandu.

Meanwhile, the Nepalese government was also under pressure. It needed to pacify China, but was powerless to stop the Khampas. Desperate, it closed the kingdom to outsiders, and suppressed all reports of guerrilla activities. Support from the CIA ran out in the early 1970s, when President Nixon's visit to China relaxed Sino-American relations. Still, the Khampas fought bravely on, surrendering only in response to a taped plea from the Dalai Lama, and a brutal campaign by the Nepalese army.

In the mid-1970s, the government of Nepal moved into Lo with extensive plans for development and cultural integration. The area below Kagbeni was opened to tourism, but the upper reaches remained sealed. Although small-scale improvements such as elementary schools, health posts, and the installation of water pipes were popular, very little was done to compensate for the economic decline of the area caused by the closure of its borders. In fact, the real effect was more insidious: with the new schools stressing Hindu ideology, and an influx of police and aid

workers from the lowlands, the government was aiming to draw the Tibetan Buddhists of Lo into the Nepalese mainstream. The nationalistic fervor of the Panchayat system, which proposed a great Hindu kingdom united by the Nepalese language, handed the people of Lo a double-edged sword: was the economic need for a recognized Nepalese identity to be achieved at the expense of an ancient way of life?

At heart a tough community of farmers and traders, the "Lo-pas" (as they call themselves) have always had to adapt to survive; but never before have they faced such a threat to the very building blocks of their society. While the closure of upper Mustang to a large extent preserved a microcosmic version of old Tibet, it left the population poor, marginalized, and unable to benefit from the tourist dollars and foreign aid pouring into the rest of Nepal. The challenge—as the first wave of trekkers discovers the "forbidden kingdom"—will be to accommodate local, national, and foreign needs without further compromising its rich but fragile culture.

Page 20: Looking north from Kagbeni
Page 21: Ame Pal's fortress of Ketchen Dzong towers above Lo Manthang.
Left: Stupas and sacred stones protect travelers from the perils of the journey.

2

Journey to Lo Manthang

Unless one charters a helicopter, the only viable means of reaching Mustang today is the traditional one, which follows the old salt route up the Kali Ghandaki Gorge. Traders of a bygone age would make the long ascent on foot, their mules laden with grain, rice, and small luxuries from the lowlands. Nowadays most people, including locals, travel as far as Jomsom in one of the small Twin Otters that shuttle daily from Pokhara and Kathmandu. It is a journey of breath-taking beauty. Flying only in the early morning, to avoid the crippling north wind that whips up the gorge from about eleven onward, the planes head northwest along the main wall of the Annapurna massif. Gradually, green terraces give way to a stark rockscape washed clean by the elements. High above, row upon row of majestic snow peaks reach unimaginably into the sky. There

is little sign of vegetation or settlement: this barren land does not bend easily to the will of man.

The approach is hair-raising. Planes can easily be lost in bad weather, their pilots unable to find the narrow gap at fifteen thousand feet, which forms the gateway to the dirt airstrip at Jomsom. Passengers disembark into another world. Despite a haphazard array of modern buildings, the core of the village is of traditional Tibetan design. Horses saddled with brightly woven carpets, and mules with bells at their throats are tethered along the main street. They wait patiently to be loaded for onward journeys, which today are more likely to involve travelers than trade. Townsfolk and tourists negotiate with sherpas in flip-flops. Darting between them are bright-eyed Tibetan girls from the refugee camp at Marpha. Inveterate traders, they

walk for hours each day to sell trinkets to the trekkers. Unlike their fellow exiles in the valleys though, they no longer look incongruous in this environment.

Jomsom is a town in transition. Its position at the crossroads of major trekking routes, and the recent addition of the airstrip, have given it a prominence not warranted by history. Despite its schools, lodges, aid organizations, army base, and field hospital, it maintains the air of a frontier town, straddling borders of time and tradition. Gone are the pagoda-like stupas of the lowlands. Here, Buddhist *chortens* colored red

and ocher like the rocks testify to an altered sensibility. The pole of orientation has begun to shift toward Lhasa.

At the edge of town, the trail crosses a small suspension bridge, and immediately enters the Kali Ghandaki Gorge—the deepest canyon on earth. A vast, rock-strewn chasm, it follows the great Himalayan breach, cutting right through the highest part of the massif. The peaks of Nilgiri (23,166') and Tukuche (22,703'), which rise directly above the river bed, bound the horizon with an immensity that seems to transcend physical contours to become spiritual.

Page 24: A Hindu pilgrim returns from the sacred shrines of Muktinath.
Page 25: High mountain pass at Samar
Page 26: Horses, often used to carry trekkers' supplies, cross a narrow footbridge.
Above: On leaving Jomsom, travelers enter the Kali Ghandaki Gorge.

It is no surprise that the Kali Ghandaki is thought to be sacred. For Hindus, this is the domain of Kali the Black, the goddess of death and destruction. Since time immemorial, travelers have carried the fossilized ammonites found here as charms against her wrath. The teachings of the Buddha however, are more pragmatic: Tibetans believe that the great mountains themselves were once an ocean. The fossils serve to remind us of the mutability of all things. Modern science identifies this area as the ancient Sea of Tethys, destroyed when the collision of India with the Eurasian continent formed the Himalayas.

Some three-and-a-half hours' walk from Jomsom, the village of Kagbeni, with its small skirt of fields, nestles into the rocky moraine beside the river. Forming at one time the southernmost boundary of the kingdom of Lo, it is still a major crossroads for traders, trekkers, and pilgrims. To the east lie the sacred shrines of Muktinath, Thorung La, and the Annapurnas. The difficult westward route leads to Dolpo. At the end of the village, next to the police post, stands a battered metal sign. Its message is at once intransigent and wildly alluring: RESTRICTED AREA. NO ONE BEYOND THIS POINT. Ahead, the trail winds northward, along the flanks of the Kali Ghandaki, toward the heart of the forbidden kingdom.

More than a thoroughfare, Kagbeni is also an important cultural pivot. Until 1992, it was the end of the line. Now, it is the first of thirteen hamlets known as "Baragaon." Within the Nepalese administration, the district of Mustang is divided into four zones, reaching from Thak Sat Sae in the south, up to the Tibetan border.

Although this places the official boundary of Lo as far north as Gilling, the kingdom's religious and ethnic integrity stretches much further. From Kagbeni onward, the local "Thakali" language gives way to a dialect closely resembling high Tibetan, and Buddhism breathes in every stone. Marking the entrance to the village, a large chorten straddles a stream. Inside, it is painted with *mandalas* and *boddhisattvas* — among them the religious patriarch Guru Rinpoche himself. Here, the twentieth century has made few inroads. On cobbled streets, children and woolly calves jostle for playroom. Wizened women emerge from doorways, bearing trays of *chang* and Tibetan tea. Inside, their houses are as dusty as the mountains, smelling of sweat, soot, and the pungent aroma of yak dung burning.

From Kagbeni northward, the Kali Ghandaki is dotted everywhere with small settlements. Despite the searing wind, and the obvious hardships of isolation, these villages are relatively prosperous. Places like Tangbe, Chhuksang, and Tsuk are able to harvest two crops per year: chiefly buckwheat and barley. Other sustenance comes from corn, apples, and kitchen gardens. With their neatly terraced fields, monasteries, and whitewashed dwellings, they seem like oddly ordered oases amid the chaotic drama of the landscape.

Page 28: Women of the village peer at passers-by.
Detail: The sign at the edge of Kagbeni that marks
the entrance to the restricted zone
Above: Children prepare for a festival in the narrow
cobbled streets of Ghemi.

Above: The village of Drakhmar, which means
" red cliffs," surrounded by a patchwork of fields
Page 31: Mud houses in the village of Chhuksang

Above: The village of Garphu built by the site of the ancient cave dwellings
Page 33: The monastery at Tangbe

At last the canyon narrows, and the river disappears into a ravine. Crossing a perilous footbridge, travelers are forced upward, toward the windswept aerie of Tsele. From every rooftop, strings of prayer flags ward off demons and landslides. Above, carved so high into the rockface as to seem completely inaccessible is a cluster of sixteen caves, which once contained the *Sacred Texts of Hum*. Representing the essence of the Tibetan wisdom teachings, these volumes were placed in the cliffs to protect all sentient beings crossing the river.

Beyond Tsele, one reenters the gorge, climbing up a narrow track cut directly into the rock face. It becomes immediately obvious why horses and mule trains wear bells: one false step means falling hundreds of feet into the river below. Here and there, small piles of stones inscribed with mantras serve to focus the mind. Locals believe that since collective karma was responsible for the perils of this pathway, only prayer can ensure safe passage. At the top of the pass, the landscape becomes broader and more fertile. This is one of the greenest areas in Mustang, and a prime source of firewood. The village of Samar, with its broad stream and grassy slopes, was the headquarters of the Khampa army in the 1960s. When the government offered Nepalese nationality and financial incentives to those surrendering their arms, a number of soldiers stayed on, intermarrying with the local community, and becoming absorbed into society.

Page 34 Top: The sixteen caves in the cliffs at Tsele once contained
sacred texts to protect travelers.
Page 34 Bottom: Traders pass through a narrow canyon.
Above: Lamas on their way to pray at the temple of Champa Lakhang
in Lo Manthang

The steep ascent continues. Each col carries a prayer flag and a mound of sacred *mani* stones chiseled with the ubiquitous mantra: "Om mani padme hum." On the way one passes the lone teahouse of Bhena, and the forlorn settlement of Syngboche. These wayside inns are a welcome relief from the rigors of the road. Travelers meet here to take refreshment, swap stories, and play cards. Although the stake may only be a few rupees, gambling is a national obsession: no one will pass up the chance of a game.

The pass before Gilling is appropriately marked with a *chorten*. From here, the view stretches deep into the heart of Lo. Ahead lies a monolithic wasteland of mountains reaching endlessly upward and north into Tibet. It is difficult to comprehend that a culture of such richness could have blossomed in the folds of this unyielding rockscape. Gilling itself is a spacious village dominated by two *gompas*, both of the Ngorpa sect—a subsidiary of Sakya. The lower monastery has been significantly restored, and sports an array of new frescoes. In a culture where art is an expression of religious tradition, there is no special reverence for the old. Modern acrylic replacements are treated with as much pride as the original paintings.

High on the rocks above perches the little Gongkhang chapel. This is the abode of Gilling's protective gods, whose task is to do battle with the multitude of evil spirits that threaten daily life. There are, of course, many ways of dealing with demons: charms made of goats' skulls, and brushwood adorn most village houses, and mani stones stand guard above their doors. An apocryphal story tells how Guru Rinpoche chased and killed the demoness who once held sway over Lo. Where she fell, her intestines became the great prayer wall east of Ghemi, while her head, heart, and lungs are buried in a trio of chortens further up the valley.

Page 36: From the monastery at Tsarang the view stretches into the mountains of Tibet.
Above: An abandoned village on the road to Lo Manthang

As one penetrates deeper into the kingdom, reminders of a more prosperous past are everywhere. Ruined villages lie here and there along the trail, their houses fallen and their fields deserted. Only the odd, disheveled shrine stands guard against the elements. Entering Tsarang, Mustang's "second city," this theme continues. The huge chorten gate, rising proudly before it, contrasts starkly with the crumbling palace behind.

Architecturally, Tsarang follows a common pattern. Narrow streets punctuate adobe houses, their roofs stacked with precious firewood. Livestock are corralled in adjoining yards, or brought into the stables that form the ground floor of every house. A tree-trunk ladder leads up to a gallery, around which the main rooms are arranged. Family life centers on the kitchen. Women cook on open fires or mud-brick stoves, the smoke mingling with the buttery smell of Tibetan tea, and dispersing through a hole in the ceiling. Rising seamlessly from the beaten earth floor, adobe benches covered with carpets skirt the walls. Used as seats during the daytime, they become beds as darkness falls. The roof, again reached by a ladder, is used for drying dung and chilies, as a children's playground, for courtship, for solitude. Most homes also have a chapel, which houses the family shrine, ritual objects, and sacred texts. Photographs of the Dalai Lama are everywhere. More than a religious leader, he is regarded as a hero and revered as the living Buddha. Interwoven at every level, faith is the foundation that underpins the community and informs the rhythms of daily life.

Pages 38-39: Tsarang's great chorten gate
Left: Small villages such as Tsuk cling to the banks of the Kali Ghandaki.
Below: Rooftops dotted with prayer flags in Lo Manthang

The monastery at Tsarang is one of the most beautiful in the kingdom. Dating from the time of Ame Pal, it is adorned with fifteenth-century frescoes of extraordinary detail and accomplishment, and contains a priceless collection of *thangkas* and statues. Tapering elegantly in its shadow stands the palace. Although uninhabited for the past sixty years, it is redolent with reminders of a bygone age. This was once the greatest library in Lo, and still has a superb collection of sacred texts, their volumes kept between intricately carved covers, and in one case inscribed entirely in gold leaf. In contrast, the armory boasts a rather bedraggled collection of weapons, and one blackened human hand. Said to be that of the master builder, it was severed by the king after his death and kept in the palace as a memorial to his skills.

Leaving Tsarang, the trail winds through fields to the valley's edge. From here, it is only a day's walk to the Tibetan border, and a mere four hours to Lo Manthang. Looking back, the little town is silhouetted against the entire north wall of the Annapurna massif: a forbidding barrier behind which Mustang maintains its uneasy seclusion.

Page 42: A monk outside of Tsarang monastery
Left: Detail of a temple mural
Below: The monastery at Tsarang is among the most
important places of worship in the kingdom.

Much has been written about Ame Pal's capital, but it is perhaps the sense of isolation that is most palpable. From the primitive helipad at the entrance to the valley, the barren plain below seems much like any other. Then the eye refocuses to discern in the distance a tiny walled city, rising almost imperceptibly from the rubble. Above it, like an extravagant sandcastle, the ruined fortress of Ketchen Dzong testifies to the passage of time. The town itself stands as a living anachronism, in dogged opposition to the ravages of a changing universe.

Structurally, Lo Manthang has changed little since the fifteenth century, and must rank as one of the world's most unspoiled medieval cities. With the exception of the school, the police post, a few store yards, and the dwellings of the outcasts down by the river, the entire population lives within the town walls. More than a hundred tightly packed houses fill most of the available space, separated only by the boundaries of brushwood and prayer flags on each rooftop. A maze of alleys runs through them—in places only wide enough for one person to pass. Although these conditions are desperately crowded, only noble families are allowed three stories: commoners must make do with two.

Surprisingly, considering its small size, Lo Manthang is divided into four quarters, each overseen by a district headman. The most desirable, of course, is that which surrounds the royal palace, near the town gate and the main square—the focal point of urban life. The poorest houses cluster wanly around the back of the huge and imposing temples of Thugchen and Champa Lakhang. Despite social differences however, the community is united in an immovable faith. Lo Manthang's three gompas, plus the large monastery of Namgyal just across the river, are patronized by everyone, and maintain a wide spectrum of ceremonies and festivals.

Physically though, the village is clearly impoverished. From the great fissures in the town walls to the dusty mandalas in Champa Lakhang and the moisture-damaged frescoes at the Thugchen temple, Lo Manthang is desperately in need of restoration. The people of Mustang have lived so long in isolation that they have become both economically and culturally demoralized. Tradition forged a coherent community, whose value system remained constant over generations. With outside contact, and the shift of political authority toward Kathmandu, has come a sense of dislocation. Like the palace itself, the old feudal structures seem slowly to be crumbling, ruptured by ideas from another world.

Page 44: The city wall of Lo Manthang
Above: Lo Manthang, Mustang's fifteenth-century capital

3

King and Commoners

In the past, despite the restrictions of a feudal system, life in Mustang was not undemocratic. The land was too barren to support a wealthy aristocracy, so the gap between rich and poor remained small. Survival in this harsh environment demanded an interdependent society with a constant population. Individuals conformed to an established model, whose parameters were understood by everyone. Exposure to outside influences however, combined with a shift of power from local to national level, has begun to erode the old ways. The shared value system, which kept the community together for nearly a thousand years, has begun to fit more and more uneasily into the modern world. This has caused a sense of insecurity, and a surrender of responsibility at a grassroots level.

The people of Mustang are beginning to question the foundation of their lives.

This is perhaps most apparent at the top, in changing perceptions of kingship. Traditionally, the ruler of Lo was addressed as "Religious King," implying if not divine inspiration, then at least divine protection of his status. His position lay somewhere between the domain of the gods, and the office of village headman. At the very least, the king was the undisputed leader of a community whose lifeblood was religion. Intermarriage between the royal house and the aristocracy of Lhasa accented the "otherness" of the ruling family, and reinforced ties with the motherland. But the king was also one of the people. From his palace in Lo Manthang, he oversaw the daily life of a realm in which none of the major settlements were

Page 46: King Jigme Palbar Bista
Page 47: The old palace in Tsarang
Above: The King's current palace
Page 49: Horses are outfitted with brightly colored woven carpets.

more than two days' ride away, and where every village was interlinked by kinship and culture. His word was absolute, but informed by the similarity of his life with those of his people.

Today's ruler, Jigme Palbar Bista, still enjoys the love and respect of the populace, but his status has become uncertain. Robbed of his former authority when Nepal became a constitutional monarchy in 1951, his role is increasingly symbolic. Feudal privileges are retained out of respect rather than duty: the king of Mustang must now bend to the will of Kathmandu. Any social unrest is fueled by the Nepalese police force stationed in Lo Manthang, in an effort to pull the Lo-pas into the Hindu mainstream. To the police, Mustang is an unpopular posting in a backward place, plagued by the wind and inhabited by peasants. In practice, the police have minimal jurisdiction in Lo. Although they would like to relegate the king to a tourist attraction, he remains for now the people's choice, united with his subjects by tradition and language.

His staunchest support comes from the aristocracy. Mainly relatives of the royal family, these multi-cultural nobles are members of the elite "Kudak" class, whose status equals that of Nepal's ruling clan. Although adopting the Nepali name "Bista" to facilitate dealings with the government, their cultural orientation is Tibetan, and ideally they still prefer to marry Lhasan nobility. Educated in India and Kathmandu (even the girls are sent to Jomsom), their world is a cosmopolitan mixture of trade and travel. It is also an exclusive network of fam-

ily connections, nurtured by common interest, maintained by money, and upheld by tradition. With their Ray-Bans and their baseball caps, their strings of horses and their sophisticated airs, the Bistas exude confidence and power. As the kingdom's major landholders, they employ many of their neighbors, and preside over village gatherings and festivals.

Political isolation did not put the Lo-pas entirely beyond the reach of the modern world, but only the nobility had the means, contacts, and leisure to generate much outside income. Since Mustang was opened, they have been the first to benefit from tourism by providing lodges, hiring out ponies, and acting as guides or interpreters.

Prosperity though, especially during hard times, can bring unpopularity, and the Bista clan is no exception. As Mustang moves toward a cash-based economy, the rift between rich and poor is growing. Old schisms widen as the political focus shifts from local to national power bases, and communal responsibility gives way to individual gain. The supremacy of the Bistas was always acknowledged, but accepted in the context of a community where everyone's understanding of life shared the same framework. Today, reinforced by education and experience far beyond the reach of the peasantry, it is no longer so easily tolerated.

Farmers form the majority of the population. They either till their own fields, or work for the king and the aristocracy. The basic unit of society is the household. Traditionally, each family was obliged to pay taxes to the realm in the form of service. Despite Mustang's entry into Nepalese party politics, many still observe the old customs. In this way, the community remains practically involved in its own maintenance.

On another level, mutual dependence is reflected in the system of village headmanship. Recruited either by household rotation or common consent, the headman and his deputies are responsible for the smooth running of village affairs. Duties include maintaining irrigation channels, deciding which common pastures can be grazed, fining the owners of straying animals, and settling disputes. Posts are held annually, and abuses of power are rare: it is hard to deal too severely with your neighbors and friends.

Survival in Lo has always depended on a stable population divided into self-sufficient units. This has called for a flexible attitude toward marriage, so as to avoid breaking up the family land. Although the Lo-pas do practice polygamy if the first wife is infertile, the most common solution is fraternal polyandry. If two or more brothers marry the same woman, then the farm need not be split among them. Moreover, they will not produce an insupportable number of children, so the ratio between people and resources will remain constant. Although the oldest brother becomes the official head of the household, this hierarchy is not very rigid in practice. Children are treated equally, and refer to both men as "father."

Polyandry worked for generations in a culture where social responsibility, and the Buddhist ideal of non-attachment, were more important than personal preference. Unmarried men and women became monks and nuns, thus perpetuating the monastic tradition, and further easing pressure on the land. Inevitably, this is changing as Mustang moves into the modern world. Although marriage is still regarded to a large extent as a social duty, most people now make monogamous marriages, based at least in part on love.

A similar tension between personal and public gain is evident in religious life: becoming a monk in Mustang has always had more to do with destiny than vocation. Unless recognized as a *tulku*, the reincarnation of a deceased lama, a child is normally selected for monkhood by his family. Traditionally, second sons were sent to the monasteries, while elder and younger children were groomed for farming and commerce respectively. The novice would be registered at the local lamasery (Buddhist seminary) around the age of nine, and though continuing to live at home, would be tutored by the monks until old enough to enter the religious community. From then on, he was free to decide which vows he would take, and under which lamas he would study. This would often involve pilgrimages to other monasteries to learn from great teachers.

Inevitably, recent history has affected this practice. Since the Chinese invasion stopped the exchange of lamas and learning between Mustang and Tibet, scholars have migrated south to Kathmandu, or to the new monasteries established by Tibetan exiles in India. Nonetheless, religious life continues to serve an important, if reduced, role—as an economic safety net, and as the inspirational force within the social order. The relationship between monastery and village is reciprocal, and benefits everyone. Monks are paid by the community to perform the religious ceremonies that form the backbone of daily life. In return, the monastic fraternity absorbs younger sons and unmarried daughters, and provides for the poorest families by allowing them to cultivate its fields, in return for a portion of the harvest.

Page 51 Top: Monks officiating at a religious ceremony to mark the King's visit to the Namgyal monastery
Page 51 Bottom: The King and Rinpoche at Lo Gekhar, Mustang's oldest monastery
Pages 52 & 53: Although much of Mustang's population migrates in winter, small bands of nomads live permanently on the high plateau.

At the bottom of the social order in Mustang are three groups who live outside orthodox village life. Although much of the population migrates in winter, a small number of nomads live permanently on this part of the Tibetan plateau—moving only to find fresh pasture for their yak herds. Regarded as uncouth by their settled neighbors, they are nonetheless deeply religious. Every tent has a family altar, and their lives are bound by the same traditions as the rest of the populace. Buddhist principles also account for two classes of outcasts who, although providing indispensable services, are forced to live on the fringes of society. The *shembas*, or butchers, slaughter livestock for meat, without involving fellow villagers in the negative karma incurred by taking life. Similarly, the *garas*, or blacksmiths, are thought to anger the spirits by taking metals from the earth. Despite their low status however, both classes interact with the community on a daily basis.

Page 54 & Right: Children roam throughout the village.
Above: Garas (blacksmiths) firing horseshoes

In every respect, the traditional order stressed close social ties as a means of managing limited resources. The need for this remains today, despite the relentless pressure to embrace a pan-Nepali value system. But what of the future? How will the children of Mustang balance their cultural heritage with the demands of the new technological age? Ironically, education—which should hold the key to the problem—is currently causing not only confusion, but increased polarization from which the society may not easily recover. In the old order, everyone who could speak had a voice in the community. Reading was left to the monks: with the exception of the lamaseries, the traditional culture had no schools. Knowledge was absorbed from family, village, and environment. Even the Bista children grew up within this framework: learning that was not religious had little relevance to daily life.

Page 56 & 57: Youngsters grow up as part of an extended family that spans several generations; villagers form a tightly knit community.
Pages 58 & 59: The village of Namgyal

Today of course, everything has changed. The sons of the nobility go away to colleges in Kathmandu and India. They return with fluent English and a sophistication that equips them for the modern world, but breeds impatience with the traditional lifestyle. For the peasantry there are fewer options. Those parents who see the value of literacy send their children to one of the elementary schools in the larger villages run by the Nepalese government. Here they are taught basic skills—but so far only in the Nepali language. Pupils are given Hindu names by teachers from the lowlands, and grow up with a diluted understanding of their culture, unable to write the language they speak at home.

Many of the poorer families do not pursue even this course. Seeing no benefit in formal education (particularly for girls) they keep their offspring at home. Although conversant with tradition, these children are condemned forever to remain at the bottom of the socioeconomic pile, lacking the skills with which to benefit from the changes affecting their community.

Evidently, present educational options in Mustang are socially divisive, reflecting a trend away from the old order. Although existing structures are falling apart, there is no coherent system with which to replace them. Society is becoming increasingly polarized, resulting in factionalism and discontent. As the gulf between rich and poor becomes a question not only of wealth but of culture, the Lo-pas stand uneasily on the threshold of a world whose possibilities may benefit only a few.

4
Rites of Passage

In contrast to the western concept of life as a road, Buddhists understand existence to be circular: a wheel of constant returning, in which death in this life merely prepares us for birth in the next. Our present experience is therefore both the result of past actions, and the cause of future ones. Living and dying have no absolute value. They are just stages in a perpetual cycle of becoming, whose upward or downward spiral is the responsibility of each individual, and ultimately of the whole community.

This world view lies at the heart of family life in Mustang. It all begins before conception, as the soul of the unborn is drawn toward existence by desire. The consciousness of the child-to-be then becomes attracted to parents whose karma is similar to its own. The elements gather

together, and a baby is conceived. After the birth, mother and child remain at home for several days, to protect the infant from evil spirits. Naming is a matter for the local lama, and may be delayed for up to a year: in a society without primary health care, neonatal death is a common and accepted fact of life. Most women expect to lose at least one child in infancy.

Children are universally adored by the Lopas, and are looked after by the whole household. From the moment they are born they are in constant contact with others, slung in a shawl on the back of a relative by day, and sleeping in their mother's arms at night. Daily care is shared by both men and women, and children are always included in every gathering. As soon as they are able, little ones are expected to contribute their share: fetching

water, gathering dung, or carrying their younger siblings on their backs. In this way, they participate in the daily life of the community from an early age, and grow up as part of a web of relationships spanning several generations.

The interdependence of the family unit is maintained into maturity, and takes precedence over all other partnerships. Nonetheless, young adults do have some room to maneuver. A relatively relaxed sexual code gives young men at least, a measure of freedom. Marriage, rather than sexual activity, is seen as the gateway to grown up life. Although divorce is permissible and without undue stigma, attitudes among the young are generally fatalistic: romance may be fun, but marriage is a duty to family and farm.

Page 60: It is a great honor to be blessed by a high lama.
Page 61: The Temple of Thugchen in Lo Manthang
Page 62 & Above: Children are universally adored by
the Lo-pas, and are looked after by the entire household.

*Page 64 Top & Above: Older children lend a hand with
younger siblings.*
*Page 64 Bottom: Western influence infiltrates in many
ways. Here a woman has forsaken traditional garb.*

Above: Women wear their finest clothes for religious festivals.
Right: The perak is an elaborate turquoise headdress, passed from mother to daughter.
Page 67 Top: Men on the groom's side of the family arrive to collect the bride for her wedding.
Page 67 Bottom: Women dancing at a wedding celebration

An alliance requires the consent of both families and the local astrologer, who also fixes the most auspicious date for the wedding. On the day itself, the bride leaves her father's house garlanded with *khatas* and crowned with her mother's *perak*, an elaborate turquoise headdress worn both as adornment and to indicate wealth. Traditionally, a woman passes her jewels to her eldest daughter upon marriage, to ensure that she will retain her own share of the family assets. A large procession gathers to escort the girl to her new home: it is important for the whole village to witness the event and mark its passing. On the threshold of the bride's new life stands a lama, who throws rice at her to make certain she brings no evil into the house. This is the only time a monk is involved. Marriage is seen as a secular ritual—a deal to be made between families. In taking her place at her husband's side, a wife assumes her new position among his people. Only the dowry (usually livestock or a field) and the reception remain. Often lasting several days, this is a grand affair that involves singing, dancing, feasting, and copious quantities of alcohol.

After the wedding, life resumes its normal pattern and the household hierarchy adjusts to accommodate the new status of the married son—who normally begins to take over leadership of the family at this time. Where there is no male heir, land is inherited by the eldest daughter; her husband—or husbands—having no formal jurisdiction over the family's holdings.

Life expectancy in Mustang is low (about fifty years), but those who survive childhood are generally active and relatively fit until the day they die. Illness is attributed to bad karma, or the influence of evil spirits. The medical system that has evolved in response to this is necessarily rooted in religious tradition—with a spicing of shamanistic ritual catering to popular superstitions. Adapted from Ayurvedic, Graeco/Arab, and Chinese sources, Tibetan medicine is an inductive and intuitive form of healing. The body is believed to be a microcosmic version of the activity of the universe: the five elements of the outside world—earth, fire, water, air, and space—having active counterparts within the body. Any imbalance between them causes disease. Unlike his western counterpart, the *amchi* (Tibetan doctor) does not use instruments for diagnosis, but relies instead on subtle pulse readings and the analysis of urine. Surgery is unknown. Cures are effected through the use of traditional medicines, blood-letting, massage—and of course prayer.

Unsurprisingly, it is common for the local doctor to be a lama. Tashi Chusang, the amchi of Lo Manthang, additionally acts as astrologer and painter, positions to which he was appointed by the king. An unassuming man in his sixties, he is known as one of the most eminent herbalists in Nepal. Villagers knock on his door at all times of the day and night, confident in the old man's soft-spoken wisdom. They pay what they can: a few eggs, some barley or buckwheat, a little *chang* . . . Prescriptions are holistic, commonly embracing diet and behavior, and requiring the support and belief of the whole village. In this way, the well-being of the individual is bound by karma to that of the community.

Page 68: On the outskirts of Lo Manthang, an old man prays.
Above: Thangkas, religious scroll hangings
Left: A charm made from a goat's skull is used to protect the household from hungry ghosts.

The elderly play a central role in this respect. Never marginalized, they are venerated as guardians of tradition, and participate fully in family life. At the age of sixty-four, a person (or couple, if both partners are still alive) may choose to retire from village life. A big party is held in the elders' honor, and henceforth they are released from all communal obligations. Most people though, continue to do lighter duties in the house and on the family land. Grandparents inevitably spend long hours with little children. Not only do they often form a special bond, but both benefit from constant involvement with those at the opposite end of the life cycle.

Death, when it comes, is accepted as the prelude to reincarnation. As soon as a person stops breathing, the lamas are called in. Reading aloud from the *Tibetan Book of the Dead*, they guide the departed soul on its way through the *Bardo*, the intermediate state between birth and rebirth. Only those who can see the terrors of this journey as an illusion, and turn instead toward the "clear light of the void," can escape the cycle of creation and attain *Nirvana*.

The people of Lo dispose of their dead in four ways. Each reflects a different element (fire, earth, water, or air) and all respect the sparse resources of the land. The rarest and most revered method is cremation. Since only wood is used for the pyre, this means is extremely costly, and is usually reserved for lamas. After the fire has burned out, any remaining bones are ground, mixed with clay, and shaped into the tiny votive figures found in sacred spots all over the kingdom.

The lowest forms of burial involve earth and water. If the body is to be interred, the back is broken to avoid demons. The deceased is placed upright in a shallow grave, marked by a prayer flag. When a corpse is to be cast into water, a lama accompanies the body breakers to a lonely place away from the village. Here, prayers are said, and offerings made. Using a ritual knife, the cadaver is then covered with cuts to aid predators, before being dismembered and thrown into the river.

Similar ceremonies inform the body's return to the final element: air. Though considered unpleasant, and often sensationalized by westerners, sky burial is in fact the most efficient way to dispose of the dead in this environment. Accompanied by a lama, relatives, and friends (one of whom acts as master of ceremonies), the corpse is carried to a high place where it is broken into pieces. When the skull and bigger bones have been crushed and the flesh exposed, conches are blown to summon the vultures. The deceased is never left unattended: it is a mark of disrespect to leave the burial ground before all has been consumed, and the departed soul has become one with the wind.

In all cases, the Lo-pas adopt a pragmatic approach, in which expediency coexists with Buddhism and a spirit-world of older beliefs. Infants are buried quickly with a minimum of ceremony: they have not been part of the

community long enough to require adult death rites. A first-born son however, merits special treatment. In the absence of another male heir, the child's body is preserved in salt and walled into the family home. In this way, the household will be protected from hungry ghosts until the arrival of another baby boy. Only then can the dead be dislodged and cremated. Thus the Lo-pas' concept of existence takes the finality out of dying: death is just another milestone on the way to rebirth. At the same time, it stresses the need to acquire merit through virtuous action, in a world where every living thing is interdependent, and all matter is engaged in the constant becoming of the universe.

Page 70: A monk rings bells at the festival of Lok Khor.
Page 71: Body breakers chant prayers as they prepare a corpse for a water burial.

Above: A charm made of juniper and a goat's scull is used to ward off evil spirits.
Right: Prayer flags and mani stones inscribed with the mantra "om mani padme hum"

5
Making a Living

In order to farm an upland desert, the people of Mustang have had to work together and conserve their resources. Despite the brief appearance of summer rains, the kingdom is scoured by sun and wind from May until October, before plunging into a harsh winter, which freezes everything into numb isolation for the next eight months. This climate, coupled with a mean altitude of fifteen thousand feet, severely restricts the growing season and the variety of crops—nothing at all would be possible without irrigation.

Generations ago, the Lo-pas constructed intricate networks of channels to tap the meltwater from mountain torrents and bring it down to their fields. Here, they subdivide it into a maze of smaller ditches that weave through the crops, being stopped or allowed to flow according to a strict rotational system.

Water rights are determined by means of a lottery. In a game called *chu gyen* (meaning "to win water") the name of each farmer is called out as dice roll. The household that wins the most points gets the first share of water. The second tally is next, and so on. Popular belief that the gods control this game of chance reinforces confidence in its fairness: no family will score badly forever.

In Lo, the farmer's year begins with the melting of the snows and the gradual greening of the plateau. Before the cycle can start however, the spirits of earth and water must be pacified. They are the soul of the land, and a good harvest depends upon their cooperation. Monks gather to intone prayers, as offerings are placed on mud-brick altars dotted among the fields, or thrown to the serpent deities that

inhabit the streams. Plowing is undertaken only on an astrologically auspicious day, when the elements of earth and water are ideally matched. After planting, the whole village celebrates. Archery competitions are held, and the chang flows freely.

A careful eye is kept on emerging shoots. In spring, Mustang is prone to dust storms, which whip up suddenly and cause devastating erosion. There is great concern if the rains are late. Since all agriculture is ruled by local gods, any minor disturbance can delay the monsoon and ruin the harvest. Outsiders are particularly culpable. Recent tourists have been baffled by angry accusations from the Lo-pas that they have caused a drought. Conversely, it always rains when a high lama comes to visit—such honored guests are especially welcome during the summer months.

Page 74: A trader's basket
Page 75: Livestock grazing at the village of Drakhmar
Top: Terraced fields near Tsuk
Above: A prayer-flag pole lies fallen on a pile of mani stones.
Page 77: Irrigation channels wind among the fields and occasionally right through the village of Kagbeni.

To ensure divine assistance, a festival known as "Lok Khor" is held in midsummer. Early in the morning, offerings of incense and khatas are made in the temple. Then, everyone parades around the fields, led by a senior lama, chanting prayers of aspiration for timely rains, good crops, and a dearth of insects and hailstorms. Monks form a long procession, playing horns, cymbals, and drums. The air resounds with the haunting tones of the conch and the mournful wailing of the Tibetan oboe. Each villager, from stooped old grandfather to smallest child, carries a volume of scripture. In this way, the power of the *Dharma* will protect both home and harvest.

Page 78 Top & Bottom: During a Lok Khor festival,
a procession of monks circles the village fields,
praying for timely rains.
Above: A little girl carrying sacred texts on her back
Right: Women carry Buddhist scriptures through the
fields to ensure a good harvest.

As summer tips over into fall, the skies clear, and the land glows golden with ripening barley, interspersed with startling pink fields of buckwheat. Siberian cranes curve in long arcs across the skies. Although the days are still warm and the sun burns fierce in the thin mountain air, the mornings are now chilly. At night, the temperature plummets below freezing: the snows are not far away.

Before the harvest begins however, people gather from far and wide for the races. Known as the festival of "Yar Dung," this is a hugely popular event involving archery tournaments and shows of equestrian bravado. The riders must reach down to pick up *khatas* at a gallop, fire arrows in full flight, or lean back on their moving horses, with their heads only inches from the ground. Even in a culture where children are tied onto ponies before they can walk, this calls for skill—and nerves of steel.

Left & Above: In summer, the land glows golden with
ripening barley and buckwheat.

After the festival, work begins in earnest. For the three weeks it takes an average family to harvest their fields, everyone rises before dawn and labors ceaselessly until after dark. Reapers work in long rows across the fields, cutting the crops with small sickles. Peas, barley, and buckwheat are all threshed on earthen floors. The grain is either beaten by hand with wooden paddles, or trampled by livestock driven in circles around an iron stake. Small children scurry with baskets behind the animals, picking up excrement before it can contaminate the crop. The king himself oversees the harvesting of the royal fields, and can often be seen driving his horses around the threshing yard. It is not surprising that many of his people feel that he understands their lives, and prefer his authority to that imposed by proxy from Kathmandu.

Bringing in the harvest is a time of relief and celebration. Offerings of butter lamps and *tsampa* (barley flour mixed with Tibetan tea) are placed on family altars, and everyone relaxes. As the nights draw in, men repair their homes against the coming cold, while their womenfolk prepare for the long trek south. Today, almost half the population of Lo migrates in winter in search of work; either to Pokhara and Kathmandu or even further, into northern India.

Page 82: *A green field outside of Tsarang*
Top: *Carrying heavy loads is part of everyday life.*
Detail: *The Buddha looks on as villagers participate in the Lok Khor parade.*

Since the Chinese took over Tibet, traditional trading patterns have been greatly curbed. Many Lo-pas are forced to supply labor for cash in order to subsist. The old system of barter can no longer sustain them. Nonetheless, the backbone of the old salt trade survives. Although heavily regimented by the Chinese (who control exchange rates, quotas, and trading partners), it is still possible to make a profit if one is clever. Luckily, the people of Mustang are good at business: merchandise from both sides of the border changes hands, particularly on the black market.

Left: An old woman collects yak dung, which is used as fuel to supplement meager supplies of firewood.
Below: Women work together to bale the harvest.
Page 85: A woman uses a strainer to sift barley and other grains.

Caravans travel south in late October to spend the winter in the lowlands, returning to Mustang only when the route becomes passable again in the spring. This is also the time when animals are slaughtered. Large herds of sheep and goats, fat from summer feeding, crowd noisily along the trails, bound for markets in the valleys. Livestock is essential to the lives of the Lo-pas. The inhabitants of Lo Manthang alone keep more than two thousand sheep and goats, nearly three hundred horses, and at least as many mules. In a land impassable to vehicles, animals are vital for meat, milk, wool, skins, and transportation.

In fact, some Lo-pas rely entirely on their livestock for survival. Clustered in the northern part of the kingdom, a small but tenacious group of nomadic pastoralists live solely by means of herding. A tough, dignified people, they camp all year-round in thick black tents made from yak felt. Constructed to house an entire family, these are pitched over shallow troughs, dug into the ground as protection from the bitter winds of the plateau.

Despite the hardships of such a life, the nomads have evolved a means of animal management that has allowed them to inhabit this area for centuries without exhausting their resources. Toward the end of summer, they lead their livestock away from the home pastures to a temporary encampment, left ungrazed during the growing season. When the new ground is exhausted, the household moves back to its original camp, and the herds live off the remaining vegetation there until the following spring. In this way, the animals build up stores of fat, which enable them to survive the harsh winter, without overburdening available food supplies.

Although sheep and goats form the bulk of their business, the nomads also keep a number of yaks. Unique to the Tibetan plateau, the yak is a monolithic animal. With its shaggy outer coat, soft cashmere-like undercoat and a huge subcutaneous layer of fat, it is able to withstand intense cold. Unhappy below ten thousand feet, it grazes at altitudes well beyond the reach of sheep or goats, thus avoiding competition for the same pastures. As a beast of burden the yak is unparalleled, but it also yields meat, milk, wool, and leather. Anything in excess of the family's needs is sold or bartered for other staples.

Page 86: Huge copper prayer wheels frame the gateway to Lo Manthang—a favorite gathering spot for townspeople.

Pages 86 & 87: Stone walls protect these goats from wolves and snow leopards.

Pages 88 & 89: Nomads live all year round in thick black tents made from yak felt.

Pages 90 & 91: A trader with his precious cargo of firewood.

Inevitably, the recent political climate has caused hardship for the herders. Though spared the evils of the commune, which so disastrously afflicted their counterparts in Tibet, the nomads of Lo have found their access to long-established pastures and markets restricted. Like the villagers, their ancient way of life is becoming ever more difficult to sustain.

Altogether, the prognosis for survival in Lo by traditional means is not good. Despite extreme conservation of their resources, and ingenuity in their approach to farming and trade, people are struggling. The huge winter exodus made necessary by the kingdom's closure, and exacerbated by Nepalese imports of salt from India, has caused a decline of living standards and morale. It is no wonder that the villagers of Mustang welcome tourism with open arms. Sadly, present regulations mean that locals see little of the tourist dollar. Resentment has been further fueled by the illegal profiteering of the nobility, and the inevitable rise in the price of wheat, which followed the easing of restrictions. The influx of outsiders is a burden: tourism has not yet become integrated into the yearly cycle, and so remains disruptive rather than complimentary to age-old patterns.

6

The Road to Nirvana

Man says: Time passes.
Time says: Man passes.

—Tibetan proverb

For the Buddhists of Lo, all experience is qualified by an intuition of the transient and illusory nature of the human condition. Although consciousness is understood to be the creative center of the universe, emancipation from the endless wheel of rebirth can only be achieved at the expense of the self—in meditative detachment, and active compassion for all sentient beings. Man's relationship with his environment is therefore both crucial and dynamic, since all matter is interconnected, and in a constant state of flux. Our experience of life, while valid in our deluded human condition, must also enable us to perfect our understanding of emptiness, and progress toward Nirvana.

Strictly speaking then, Buddhism is less a faith than a metaphysic, and as such underlies every aspect of life, providing a cognitive structure within which to transcend the pain of ordinary existence. Its religious practices are dedicated to the accumulation of spiritual merit. Karmic law dictates that every action produces a consequence, to which either positive or negative moral value is attached. Since the balance of these conditions determines the manner of rebirth, belief in *karma* has produced not only a sophisticated system of morality, but also a variety of means of accumulating merit.

Evidence of these pervades the landscape of  Lo, almost imperceptibly blending into every village, and encompassing the mountains themselves. Most obvious perhaps are the prayer flags, which flutter like sails from every rooftop. Printed with mantras, their messages are carried aloft in the

wind as offerings. Old banners are never removed, but left to disintegrate under new ones, which are simply placed on top of them. Similar in concept, prayer wheels contain tightly rolled scrolls of paper, inscribed with sacred texts. Varying in size from small hand-held cylinders, to the huge mechanisms found in temples, aristocratic homes, and set into the city walls of Lo Manthang, they are always spun clockwise. It is believed that every revolution of the wheel accrues the merit of a complete recitation of the

prayers within. Often, as in the village of Ghemi, they are set in a row in the central square, so people can spin them every time they pass by.

Prayers are uttered constantly, and inscribed everywhere. Small mounds of engraved and painted stones mark every pass. Merit is gained not just in the act of decorating these mani stones, and placing them by the roadside: as they sit, their sacred messages become one with the universe, safeguarding travelers and redeeming collective karma.

Chortens serve similar functions. Literally meaning "heap" or "mound," they often house the remains of lamas, and as such become objects of veneration and guardians of sacred power. Like prayer wheels, chortens vary greatly in size. At one extreme are the tiny votive offerings shaped from the ashes of deceased holy men. At the other, the great chorten gate of Tsarang stands sentinel before village and gods. Painted in the holy colors of red, ocher, and white, these distinctive structures are everywhere—rising as naturally from the earth as the mountains around them, and drawing the mind through the five elements they embody, toward enlightenment.

Religion is woven into the fabric of life to such an extent that it ceases to have a separate meaning. Art, architecture, music, and drama all exist in response to the Buddhist impulse, and all function to focus the mind on its essential nature. Each act of artistic creation becomes an act of devotion.

Thus, the beautifully wrought *thangkas*, or scroll paintings, which adorn temples and family altars, are designed to be viewed not simply for pleasure, but as imaginative aids to meditation. Similarly, the knot patterns, the rows of dots, and the swastika shapes that decorate homes and horse carpets are not merely traditional designs, but important religious symbols—used both to please local spirits and to acquire merit. The same is true of music and theater: the legends of the *Lhamo* (folk opera) retell apocryphal Tibetan wisdom tales, intended to express sacred ideology in strongly dramatic terms. Although everyone constantly mutters prayers, the sacred traditions of chanting and instrumental fanfare transform the production of sound itself into a meditation.

Page 92: *A prayer flag on top of the palace*
Page 93: *Summer fields frame the Namgyal monastery.*
Page 94: *An elaborate bronze base of a prayer flag seems to balance precariously on the roof of the royal palace in Lo Manthang.*
Page 95: *Mani stones are inscribed with prayers and placed along the trail to safeguard travelers.*
Page 96: *Monks created this exquisite sand mandala for a ceremony in Tsarang.*
Page 97: *An ornate stupa at Gilling*

If Buddhism is the wellspring of life in Mustang, it also fulfills a unifying social function. This can be seen most vibrantly in the many festivals that punctuate the year. Perhaps the most important of these is the annual demon-chasing ceremony in Lo Manthang. Usually held at the Tibetan New Year, this huge spectacle lasts four days. It is a chance for the community to gather, participate in the teachings of the Buddha, and celebrate the victory of good over evil. During the ritual, a number of "demons" dressed in hideous masks and brightly colored costumes are chased from the city, to be symbolically killed by the local abbot and his monks. The involvement of the people is crucial: both as spectators, and as actors in a cosmic drama whose reality is palpable.

The Buddha exhorted his followers to take refuge in himself, his teachings (the *Dharma*), and the *Sangha*—his ordained disciples. Originally, this meant monks, nuns, and recognized teachers. Now, it is taken to include all practitioners of the teachings. Thus, Mustang's clerical community, while fulfilling society's needs by performing essential rituals, does not really play a sacerdotal role. Monks often live at home. They take an active part in the life of the village, and visit the monastery only to say prayers, light butter lamps, or perform ceremonies. Respect is earned according to conduct and spiritual status, since religious life in Lo often has more to do with necessity than vocation.

Of course, the recent political and economic climate has had a drastic effect on monastic tra-ditions in the kingdom. Before the Chinese invasion of Tibet, there was a fertile interchange of lamas and learning between Mustang and the motherland. Children would frequently be sent to monasteries in Tibet for education—particularly if they were *tulkus*, or recognized reincarnations. Lamas crossed the border to study, make retreats, or take part in festivals. Above all, the people of Lo had access to some of the great minds of the Tibetan world.

The kingdom's closure has caused a great decline in levels of learning and religious practice. Although high lamas such as Chobje Trichen Rinpoche and Tashi Tenzing (the abbot of Lo Manthang) act as monastic patrons and teachers, there are at present relatively few monks in Lo. Families who can afford to, send their sons to lamaseries in Kathmandu and India. Generally, they do not come back. Since Tibetan is rarely taught in the village schools, levels of literacy in the mother tongue are declining. Fewer monks are now able to read the sacred canon of their faith— a great loss, as the predominant Sakya sect stresses the equal value of study and practice. In addition, many texts and priceless art treasures were removed during the Khampa period, or lost illegally in recent years to the international market.

Page 98: A gilt statue at Namgyal Monastery
Above: A young monk announces morning prayers.
Right: A high lama greets a young follower.

Nonetheless, Mustang's monasteries remain the primary symbol of its cultural heritage, and contain some of the finest examples of Tibetan religious art in the world. In Lo Manthang alone, there are four temple complexes, the oldest dating from the town's inception in the fifteenth century. All bear witness to the historical importance of Lo as a center of learning and pilgrimage.

Perhaps the most dramatic is Champa Lakhang, the "Temple of the Coming Buddha." Though much of this extraordinary, three-story building has fallen into disrepair, its effect is still breathtaking. The main hall is preceded by a large cloister, surrounded by an open gallery supported on immense wooden columns. Ahead, the tapering red-earth structure of the shrine room towers above the town. Sadly, the lower floor now lies in ruins, so the only workable entrance is at roof level, above the courtyard.

Inside, the smallish temple is overwhelmed by an enormous golden statue of Maitreya, the Coming Buddha. Countless khatas dangle in dusty knots from its arms, while its all-seeing eyes gaze out like beacons in the darkness. Until recently, this forty-five-foot colossus was the largest statue in Nepal. Huge tree-trunk beams support the ceiling. Around the walls, barely discernible in the gloom, are painted the most exquisite medieval mandalas—circular diagrams of the six realms of existence used for visualization during meditation.

Originally, Champa Lakhang contained as many as eighty mandalas, all of immense artistry, and embellished with gold leaf. Of these, roughly half have survived the passage of time. Very few paintings of this age and quality are left outside Mustang, since the systematic burning of Tibet's monasteries during China's Cultural Revolution destroyed most of its great art works. It is perhaps in response to this that UNESCO has plans to declare Champa Lakhang a world heritage site.

Page 100: Detail of a fifteenth-century gilded fresco in the temple of Champa Lakhang
Below: A statuette in front of the great Maitreya, the Buddha who is yet to come, at Champa Lakhang

Next door is the cavernous temple of Thugchen. In contrast to the airy loftiness of Champa Lakhang, a heavy door leads down from the street into darkness. Inside, the menacing forms of wrathful gods glower to left and right. Ahead lies an elegant hall of classical Tibetan design. Illuminated by a single skylight, this vast space is interrupted only by a colonnade of square carved pillars, behind which pockets of darkness seem to lurk like watchful spirits. At the far end, butter lamps flicker on the altar, illuminating rows of gilt bronze statues. Of varying size, they represent manifestations of the Buddha, *Mara*, and the great Tibetan saints. Originally, the temple walls were decorated with huge paintings, depicting the five Buddhas of Universality, but these are now badly decayed.

Unfortunately, Thugchen has suffered severe water damage in recent years, which has destroyed many of the fine frescoes and much of the woodwork. The local community has made huge efforts to repair their temple, but available resources are inadequate. Despite layers of mud added to the ceiling, and the rebuilding of the entire north wall, moisture still seeps in elsewhere. Recently, the Nepalese government stepped in with a small grant, but this has proven to be woefully inadequate. The great religious buildings of Mustang continue to crumble.

Although both Thugchen and Champa Lakhang are used regularly, the main activities of the monastic community center around the "new" monastery of Choedhe, and Namgyal—a larger complex just outside the city walls. The former has two main temples: the first houses the colorful masks used in the demon-chasing festival, the second contains more exquisite medieval frescoes. Similar in quality and style to those in the monastery at Tsarang, they are richly wrought depictions of the religious pantheon.

Thanks to the efforts of local monks, a small lamasery is about to open at Choedhe. Funded by Sakya charities in India and Nepal, it will initiate some thirty-five students into religious life, using Tibetan as its language of instruction. In addition to their regular studies, selected pupils will also learn the art of traditional medicine from the amchi Tashi Chusang and his son.

Page 102: The courtyard of the Choedhe monastery in Lo Manthang
Above: A gilt statue of the Buddha inside a chamber in the old palace

Below Top: Sacred texts are often kept inside stupas.
Below Bottom: Conch shells are widely used in religious ceremonies.
Right: The Namgyal monastery, north of Lo Manthang

 Of course, Lo Manthang was never the only center of monastic achievement in Lo. Scattered throughout the kingdom, numerous temples contain reminders of Mustang's rich traditions. The oldest of these is Lo Gekhar, which stands alone on a hill, about three hours southwest of the capital. Dating from the latter part of the eighth century, it was built by the father of Tibetan Buddhism, Padmasambhava. According to legend, the site became a holy place when a spring bubbled up where the saint's tears fell.

Constructed over a smaller shrine, its five rooms are decorated with intricate wall carvings. Inside the main chapel, a huge statue of Maitreya sits meditatively behind a multitude of butter lamps. The holiness of the place is immediate and intense. Although it once housed a sizable community, the temple is now maintained only by a couple of caretaker monks. Still, it remains a place of pilgrimage and special reverence for the people of Lo.

Perhaps the most extraordinary places of worship in the kingdom are its cave networks, hollowed inaccessibly high into the cliffs at Yara. Carved out by hand, they were reached by

Page 106: A temple in the village of Garphu, north of Lo Manthang, in an area that is now restricted to foreigners
Detail: Monasteries are decorated in the sacred colors of red and ocher; the paint is thrown down the walls from a bucket on the roof.
Below: High lamas travel on horseback.

Above: Prayer flags flutter from the rooftop of the temple of Champa Lakhang in Lo Manthang.
Left: A sacred text
Page 108 Top: White khatas are draped over religious statues as offerings.
Page 108 Bottom: Bound texts in the palace at Tsarang

ladders and narrow pathways. Where even these means proved impossible, logs were driven into the cliffs to make steps. In places, their pegless holes are still visible. Little is known about the hermits who lived here. Dating mostly from the fourteenth and fifteenth centuries, these caves remain one of Mustang's most tantalizing mysteries.

The majority of course, are abandoned, their front walls eroded away. High in the rockface of a forgotten chasm however, perches the extraordinary cave monastery of Lori. In its heyday, it was home to scores of monks. Today, a lone attendant visits periodically to maintain the altar and say prayers. Access is perilous. The visitor must climb almost vertically upward, across deep gorges spanned by bridges made of tree trunks. All around, sharply tapering cliffs, like primeval skyscrapers, cast bizarre shadows into the valley.

The entrance to the chapel lies through a man-made tunnel, and up an old ladder. Only two of the interconnecting chambers remain intact. The first has the orientation of a traditional Tibetan chapel—with an altar, statues, and thangkas. Beyond is a domed shrine room, filled so completely by a large chorten that only a narrow pathway remains for pilgrims to walk around. Every available surface is whitewashed and decorated with frescoes. Lori is unique: no other chortens of this age and quality have existed in man-made caves since Tibet's treasures were reduced to rubble by the Chinese.

Above: The cave monastery of Lori Gompa
Page 111 Top: Frescos adorn the walls of Lo Gekhar, the oldest temple in Mustang.
Bottom: A statue of the Buddha, and other religious artifacts, inside Lori Gompa
Page 112: The King and Rinpoche
Page 112&113 Namgyal Monastery

The people of Lo are increasingly concerned about foreign interest in their religious heritage. Despite recent restrictions imposed by the Nepalese government, the "discovery" of Mustang's temples has resulted in a large spate of thefts. Even attempts to catalog works of art are now thwarted by the locals, who fear this will only increase the likelihood that they will be stolen. Nonetheless, the monasteries of Lo are in urgent need of restoration. The involvement of the community in this process will be imperative, if the emblems of a living faith are not to become museums.

In the end though, the Buddhist ethic transcends any material monument. It lives in the mountains, is borne on the wind, and finds expression in the lives of the Lo-pas. Every individual spends a significant amount of time in meditation: whether chanting, muttering mantras, or in silence during the long walks from village to village. Never an optional extra, religion is the organizing principle of life—as crucial to people's identity as the air they breathe.

7

Conserving the Wilderness

Mustang ranks among the most unspoiled wilderness areas in the world. In this respect, its long closure has been beneficial: the kingdom has remained a remote environment, untouched by the modern world. Neighboring areas have been less fortunate. In Tibet, the Chinese have caused untold damage in the name of progress. Regions of Nepal that have become popular with trekkers are not only facing the long-term effects of deforestation, but also the disruption caused by a continual influx of outsiders. Mustang—with its constant population (whose Buddhist beliefs demand an organic interaction with their surroundings) has remained pristine, its ecosystems unchanged for generations.

Geomorphically, this area is unique. Nudging the edge of the Tibetan plateau to the north, and folding into the Kali Ghandaki  Gorge as it slopes southward, the kingdom of Mustang bears dramatic witness to the immense forces that shaped this landscape. Sixty-five million years ago, India was separated from Eurasia by the Sea of Tethys. As the two continents converged, subduction occurred along the southern margin of Eurasia, as the thinner oceanic edge of the Indian land mass pushed its way under the thicker Eurasian crust. The continental border of the Indian plate however, was too thick to be subducted: thrust faulting along this line built the Himalayas. Originally, the Tibetan plateau was higher than the emerging mountains. Several major river systems drained the land to the south. Such was their power that they eroded their beds as fast as the mountains grew. Aided by the steep gradient, and the relatively soft sandstone left by the Tethys Sea, rivers like the Kali Ghandaki

were able to bisect the main range, cutting through thousands of feet of rock to reach the plains of India.

The continual elevation of the Himalayas began to have a dramatic effect on the weather. Originally, the northern stretches were as warm as those to the south. But when the peaks began to tower above twenty thousand feet, moist air from the plains was no longer able to reach the plateau, resulting in the formation of a high desert. The great rivers, now originating in the rain-shadow belt, received less water. Today, they flow wanly, dwarfed by their vast canyons.

The Kali Ghandaki Gorge, from Jomsom northward, illustrates this phenomenon dramatically. In places almost a mile wide, it is a wasteland of gravel. Even during the wet months of summer, the river seems oddly inadequate in its surroundings. Drought is heightened by a constant wind, which blows up daily from the southwest, to reach speeds of eighty miles per hour. Most of the villages flank the eastern wall of the canyon. This side is slightly more damp, and in Mustang even small variations in climate can make a difference to cultivation. Ascending beyond Tsele into the highlands, the slopes become ever drier. Altitude plays an increasingly important part here. With the exception of the slightly greener Samar Valley, this is an arid rockscape, punctuated only with the occasional bush of blackthorn or juniper. Hidden between the tussocks lurk tiny alpine flowers. Here and there a stunted dog rose spills onto the trail: its berries are a local delicacy in the fall.

Few animals are able to exist in this environment. Those that remain have adapted their physiology to cope with extremes of cold and elevation, evolving thicker pelts, and a more efficient use of available oxygen. Since grazing is so poor, the land can only support small numbers and limited species: they form a delicate food chain, which coexists uneasily with domestic livestock. Among the rocks are rodents—mice, marmots, and rabbits—fossicking in the cushion plants and scrubby mountain grasses. Eagles and griffon vultures ride the thermals above them, ever watchful, always ready... Mustang has few indigenous birds. Of the seventy-seven species recorded in Nepal above twelve thousand feet, only fifteen inhabit the area north of Jomsom. All are natives of the Tibetan plateau, and have not been sighted elsewhere in the Nepalese highlands.

More importantly, the Kali Ghandaki is a major flight path for migrants, on their way from Palearctic breeding grounds to winter quarters in southern Asia. Every autumn the skies are speckled with skeins of Siberian cranes. Geese, ducks, and numerous kites and buzzards also set a course through the canyon. Although the birds must cross the widest expanse of the barren plateau to the north, the route offers a clear passage through the most impenetrable part of the Himalayan massif.

For some animals however, the area's unforgiving terrain is an advantage: Mustang is home to a number of rare and endangered species. Perhaps the most bizarre of these is the bharal, or

blue sheep. Technically neither a sheep nor a goat, but possessing characteristics of both, the bharal is found only above the tree line in the most remote Himalayan uplands. Grouped into small herds, these graceful animals roam the rocky slopes, their powerful, stocky bodies well adapted for survival at high altitudes. They forage among the tussocks and juniper bushes, protected from the elements by a short coat of grey-brown hair. Males sport long, curved horns, with which they give extravagant displays during the rutting season. Both bharal and domestic sheep are hunted by several predators. Although usually too large for the jackal packs that prowl around every village by night, they frequently fall victim to wolves.

The wolf is hated throughout the kingdom. While the superior agility of the bharal may enable it to escape, the Lo-pas normally corral their livestock at night. Attacking a herd unexpectedly, a wolf will slay an animal and then bolt its kill so rapidly that the shepherd often has no time to prevent the loss. Cattle and horses are also at risk, and in rare cases wolves have even been known to hunt yak.

Page 114 Detail: An elaborate shrine of goats' sculls protects the King's palace from demons.
Page 115: Vultures nest in these bizarre cliffs at Yara.
Page: 116 &117: The vast windswept canyon formed by the Kali Ghandaki River
Page 118: A stuffed snow leopard inside the temple at Tsarang is used to ward off evil spirits.
Above: High mountain passes above the tree line are typical habitats for the bharal.

Equally feared is the snow leopard, which has acquired an almost mythical status in folklore. Even today, little is known about this most elusive of predators. Rare, shy, and withdrawn into one of the most inhospitable regions on earth, it is not easily tracked. In addition, the snow leopard's camouflage is peerless. Its silver-grey pelage, dotted with darker rosettes, allows it to blend almost imperceptibly with its rocky habitat. A solitary animal, it hunts alone, associating with other cats only to mate. Cubs, which are born in pairs in June or July, remain close to their mother until they leave to establish their own territory at two years old.

In contrast to wolves, snow leopards slaughter with precision and eat slowly. This style of hunting, combined with the animal's beauty, has given rise to widespread local myths. The abbott of Tsarang tells a typical tale: "All day, the leopard waits, crouching behind a rock. He watches the sheep and goats milling around below him. Suddenly, he leaps up, pounces, and grabs his victim from above—digging his teeth deeply into its throat. He holds on, still gripping the goat by the neck, until it falls down dead. Then, the leopard drinks its blood, becoming wild and intoxicated. Just as we humans drink arak and beer, the leopard gets drunk on blood."

In fact, snow leopards are known to kill in this way, but the wounds inflicted are usually superficial. Most victims die of strangulation. This explains why the cat holds on for so long before releasing its prey and beginning to eat—and accounts for local superstitions regarding its vampirish tendencies.

The people of Lo have an ambivalent attitude toward hunting. Officially, they abstain, since the taking of life is antithetical to their Buddhist beliefs. In practice, farmers do kill predators who molest their livestock. In September 1993, the villagers of Dhi slaughtered a snow leopard and her two cubs. As is customary, the carcasses were presented to the monastery, to atone for the death of the animals and redeem the bad karma incurred by taking their lives. Nonetheless, a growing number of snow leopards and lynx are poached for profit. Despite the international ban on trade in endangered species, their skins are sold on the black market to China. (In 1990, a fact-finding team from the United States found both adult and infant snow leopard pelts for sale in the markets of Amdo. The prices asked were as low as US $30–$50.) There is no doubt that illegal hunting is increasing. Unable to derive much profit from tourism, and finding their traditional avenues for trade cut off, the people of Lo are seeking ever more ingenious ways to make money.

Page 120: A snow leopard
Above: Even during the wet months of summer,
the river seems oddly inadequate in its surroundings.

Above: A trekker enroute to Yara stops to take a photograph.
Tourists have now penetrated deeply into the forbidden kingdom.
Page 123: Trekkers crossing the Kali Ghandaki River.
Pages 124 & 125: The snow-capped peak of Nilgiri, southeast of
Kagbeni

Tourism itself poses an enormous potential threat to Mustang's fragile ecology. Popular destinations in the Nepalese highlands (such as the areas around Mounts Annapurna and Everest), which have welcomed trekkers since the late 1950s, have suffered irreparable damage. Unsustainable pressure has been put on the natural resource base, leading to pollution, deforestation, and the disappearance of indigenous wildlife.

In 1985, the Annapurna Conservation Area Project (ACAP) was set up under the auspices of the Nepalese Ministry of Tourism, to try to reverse this trend. ACAP's approach combines environmental protection with sustainable community development and tourist management. Local people are encouraged to become involved in the process, developing small-scale conservation and alternative energy schemes in order to improve their standard of living. Crucial to the success of the program is education. Aimed both at villagers and visitors, this is intended to raise levels of awareness, and so strengthen commitment to the environment.

When the Nepalese government decided to open Mustang in 1992, ACAP's brief was extended to include the restricted area. Considering the fragile ecology of the kingdom, an initial decision was made to limit tourist numbers to two hundred per year. Strict regulations were set up to ensure that trekkers would cause minimal damage. Allowed to visit only in organized groups, foreigners were additionally required to pay royalties of US $70 per person, for every

day spent north of Kagbeni. Each party must carry all fuel and food needed for the trek, and retain the services of a government-appointed "liaison officer," who is in effect a member of the Nepalese police force. It would be his duty to see that tourists did not break the rules, or stray off the designated route. In this way, it was hoped that only responsible, well-heeled westerners would make the long journey to Lo. But the Nepalese government underestimated the attraction of this long-forbidden land. The following year, the Ministry of Tourism caved in to pressure from the big trekking agencies, and raised the quota to a thousand visitors—placing unsustainable pressure on both the local community and the environment.

Neither has had time to adapt. For hundreds of years, the people of Lo have maintained a delicately balanced relationship with the land. The sudden influx of so many outsiders, however eco-friendly, threatens to strain the existing infrastructure beyond breaking point. Environmental degradation must surely follow: as food chains are interrupted, wildlife cannot flourish, and species like the snow leopard will vanish from these mountainsides forever.

Epilogue:
Into the Future...

Change lies at the heart of the Buddhist faith. It gives meaning to life and death, and a context to experience. It inhabits the seasons, migrates with the birds, and dozes by the fireside. Change is fundamental to survival. The people of Lo have always accepted this, but applied it within a worldview based on compassion, and an understanding of the interrelated nature of all phenomena. Throughout its turbulent history, Mustang has adapted constantly to outside events, without losing its cultural identity. It survived because the traditional dialogue between people and their environment was never interrupted. With the opening of its borders and the influx of the West however, the kingdom faces potential changes that reach far beyond its current ability to absorb them. Today, as never before, the Lo-pas must re-

define their identity, and reassess their relationships with the world beyond the mountains.

In many ways, of course, the old order was far from ideal. Survival in this environment has always been hard. But society had a structure in which everyone had a place and a voice. Villagers were actively involved in the administration of their lives, and felt close to the center of power. With the decision to open Mustang to tourism has come an increased level of interference from Kathmandu. No longer in control of their own destinies, the people of Lo stand bewildered in the midst of the "development process," unable to have an overview of what is happening to their lives.

The advent of trekkers may indeed provide an economic lifeline, but its impact on local culture will be immense. Naturally, Nepal

Even gifts of money to Mustang's monasteries are forbidden. These too must be offered before entering the restricted area, to be distributed later by outsiders.

Obviously, this system affords ample scope for illegal profiteering, and causes anger and frustration among the Lo-pas. Currently, some fifty percent of the population is forced to migrate south during the winter months in order to subsist. If current prohibitions were lifted, local people would be able to substitute this journey with income generated from tourism-related activities. These could include the employment of porters and ponies, the sale of fresh vegetables, and the production of local crafts. Not only do the people of Lo possess the necessary skills and resources, but their active participation in Mustang's development will be essential in maintaining cultural morale. Indeed, the proliferation of traditional skills such as carpet making, weaving, metal casting, and *thangka* painting could contribute to an artistic revival in the area.

In addition, the Lo-pas could supplement their income by providing lodgings. Currently, all trekking in Mustang is tent-based. Tour operators pay a nominal fee to use threshing floors, yards, and roof space as camp sites. This practice is not just detrimental to the environment— once again it bars the villagers from a potential source of revenue. A network of traditional inns

supports the development of tourism. The industry generates upwards of US $65 million per year in foreign exchange. Present policies however, are unsustainable. Mustang is a wild and sparsely populated area: its carrying capacity, in social and environmental terms, is extremely small. Visitor quotas have already been raised, putting great stress on local infrastructure, and unsettling the community.

Resentment is fueled by regulations that prohibit trekkers from trading with the Lo-pas, thus depriving villagers of a traditional source of income, and preventing them from profiting directly from tourism. Although sixty percent of royalty fees are channeled back into the kingdom via ACAP, the existing rules do not allow local people to act as porters or guides, to hire out horses and mules, sell provisions, or provide any other goods or services. Instead, these must be obtained from the trekking companies in Jomsom.

has always existed in Lo, catering to traders who migrate along the salt route. Although they currently lack the facilities and standards of hygiene expected by westerners, there are plans to upgrade these hostelries to service the tourist industry. The main initiative has come from the Lo-pas themselves. Recently, members of the Bista family established the "Mustang Tourism Development Cooperative." This organization, which has representatives in every major village on the tourist circuit, aims to modify existing lodges, using capital available as grants from incoming trekking fees. An agent in Kathmandu would handle bookings so as to predict and control the distribution of visitors.

Although the restriction of tourist numbers would still be essential, the cooperative would at least be able to ensure a guaranteed income for local people. So far, ACAP's response has been positive. In support of current proposals it has instigated a scheme to educate villagers in management skills, enabling them to become more aware of the needs of western tourists. In this way, it is hoped, control of the hotel business may eventually be extended beyond the royal family, to include a broader cross section of society.

Education, in every sense, will be vital to Mustang's cultural and economic survival. For the Lo-pas, it is important that their new visitors are demystified, in order to integrate their presence as much as possible into the fabric of life. Westerners, in turn, are equally in need of cross-cultural understanding. As yet, they are often guilty of improper dress and behavior (especially at sacred sites), and of intrusive photography—not to mention the illegal acquisition of antiquities.

ACAP does its best, by providing explanatory leaflets to trekking groups. In addition, a "Mustang Museum" is planned at the foot of the trail. This idea has met with a mixed response from local people. The Lo-pas feel that establishing

such a gallery will entail the removal of art treasures from their temples, and become yet another means by which Thakalis from Jomsom can make money at Mustang's expense.

There is also considerable resentment of government regulations requiring all parties visiting Lo to be accompanied by a state-appointed "liaison officer." In practice, these men are neither physically nor culturally adapted to the mountains of Mustang. They have little respect for Buddhist customs, and antagonize both trekkers and villagers. Obviously, this fragile environment demands well-regulated tourism, but here again, local involvement could solve the problem. Liaison officers from Lo would be attuned to their environment, and could additionally act as guides. Their employment would ease the current friction between police and villagers, and the division of loyalties between the king and Kathmandu. More importantly, it would allow the Lo-pas to participate more fully in their economy, and foster a sense of pride in their heritage.

Of course, the remote and inaccessible nature of the kingdom severely restricts development. Village in-fighting, coupled with a small population and scant resources, hampers efforts to coordinate community projects. Despite outside encouragement, for example, only two hydroelectric power schemes are operational in Mustang today. The rest have been rejected at a local level, or lie abandoned due to non-repayment of loans.

Similar problems afflict ACAP's health, irrigation, and forestry programs. Local people feel pressured, and are consequently unwilling to

Page 126 Detail: Children proudly pose with the Tibetan flag.
Page 127: Prayer flags flutter in the breeze atop the palace.
Page 128: A nomadic encampment
Page 129: A woman sweeping with a crude handmade broom
Page 130: This young man is acting as an interpreter between the nomads and some trekkers.
Page 131: The great prayer wall east of Ghemi
Page 132: The high mountain village of Yara is too small to accommodate a large influx of tourists.
Page 133: A nomadic child faces an unsure future.

embrace the new technology. Moreover, ACAP's own hands are tied: its budget is too small to handle the high investment needed to implement many of its proposals. Where grants do become available, villages often lack the skills or manpower to benefit from them.

Mustang's temples are another problem. ACAP has already made limited repairs to the gompas of Thugchen and Champa La Khang, but lacks the resources to undertake major restoration. The fifteenth-century frescoes in Tsarang, Lo Manthang, Lori, and elsewhere, are decaying badly, and will not withstand the continuing influx of tourism unless protected. The same applies to the scores of medieval statues and thangkas, casually stored in uncontrolled climatic conditions. The antiquities trade poses another threat: an estimated half of the kingdom's art treasures have already been removed. A detailed survey of religious buildings and an inventory of portable artworks are essential, to prevent further losses. As a result of seasonal migration, most of Mustang's temples are left unguarded during the winter months: the Nepalese police show little interest in security. Despite the continued efforts of local monks, who employ fierce mastiffs and sleep beside their altars at night, thefts are common. Once again, this must be attributed to the trading ban, and the increasing cultural despondency caused by the present system.

Local confidence is crucial to development in Mustang. Without this, the kingdom's unique qualities will be destroyed—swamped by a relentless tide of exploitation. Already, the Buddhists of Lo feel socially disadvantaged within Nepal, their long isolation having denied them the material improvements now commonplace in less remote parts of the country. There is no doubt that they perceive the advent of tourism as a great blessing. Unless local people can retain some measure of control however, the entire infrastructure of their lives is in peril. To a large extent, this will depend on strict management of visitor numbers. Limitation of this sort has been extremely successful in Bhutan, which now enjoys the fruits of tourism without detriment to its ancient culture.

In Mustang, the volume of outsiders has already exceeded acceptable levels. The problem is most acute in the capital. Not only is Lo Manthang the certain destination of every visitor, but the nature of a walled city is such that everyone is crowded into a small space. Villagers are becoming jaded, if not openly hostile, and there is a growing begging culture among the children. Of course, the designation of Lo Manthang as a world heritage site, with all the management strategies such status implies, would go some way toward easing the situation. But the real dilemma runs much deeper. Basically, it is a question of identity and self-respect. Isolated for too long behind the high walls of political expediency, the people of Lo have become culturally insecure. As they begin to encounter the modern world, they now struggle to reconcile their Nepalese citizenship with their Tibetan heritage.

The key to the kingdom's future must lie in the balance between these poles. Since Tibet fell to the Chinese, it has obviously been in the Lo-pas' interest to strengthen ties with Nepal. In doing so, they have been drawn inexorably into the religious and political milieu of a Hindu nation. If the people of Mustang are to retain their unique way of life however, they must also nurture their Buddhist culture. For the present generation, this will mean an active involvement in the tourist industry. The Lo-pas can never hope to maintain their traditions without the resources to make their own decisions. Their offspring need appropriate education: King Jigme Palbar Bista is rightly campaigning for Tibetan school teachers. Only with an ongoing understanding of their language and customs will the children of Mustang be proud to lead their community into the twenty-first century.

Glossary of Tibetan Terms

amchi • Doctor of Tibetan medicine.

Bardo • The intermediate state between birth and rebirth.

boddhisattva • An altruistic entity who chooses to remain within the cycle of existence, to work for the welfare of all sentient beings.

Buddha • Any fully realized being—usually refers to the historical Buddha. Born as Prince Siddhartha around 600 B.C., he became enlightened while meditating under a tree in Bodhgaya, Nepal.

chang • A type of beer made from fermented millet or barley.

chorten • Buddhist religious monument, also known as a stupa.

Dharma • Generally, the teachings and doctrine of the Buddha; specifically, the true path to enlightenment and the consequent states of freedom to which it leads.

dzo • A yak/cow crossbreed common throughout the Himalayan region.

gompa • Monastery or place of worship.

Guru Rinpoche/Padmasambhava • Eighth-century master who formally established Buddhism in Tibet, along with Shantarakshita and King Trisong Detsen.

karma • The imprint of past actions on the mind, which causes our experiences.

khata • White ceremonial scarf.

lama • Tibetan Buddhist monk.

Lhamo • Traditional Tibetan opera, based on popular stories. Sung in a pharyngeal voice, they also include dialogue and comic sketches.

Lo-pa • Tibetan name for people of Mustang.

mandala • Circular diagram, painting, or model that represents a perfected state of being and perception.

mani stones • Stones bearing sacred inscriptions to safeguard travelers.

mantra • Words expressing the path to enlightenment, recited during meditation to calm and purify the soul.

Mara • The embodiment of evil, usually represented as a wrathful god.

Nirvana • Enlightenment; freedom from the cycle of existence.

"Om mani padme hum " • Mantra invoking the blessing of Avalokiteshvara, the Buddha of Compassion.

perak • Elaborate turquoise headdress worn both as adornment and to inidicate wealth.

Sacred Texts of Hum • The main body of the Tibetan canon of faith.

Sakya • One of the four principal schools of Tibetan Buddhism, which stresses study and meditation equally.

Sangha • Generally taken to mean the spiritual communities of ordained monks and nuns, this body of people can include anyone who has gained a direct insight into the true nature of emptiness.

stupa • Religious monument that often houses remains of lamas, prayer scrolls, and votive offerings; objects of veneration.

thangka • Religious scroll painting, usually depicting meditational deities.

Tibetan Book of the Dead • Tibetan Buddhist scripture used to guide the consciousness through the intermediate state between death and rebirth, known as the Bardo.

tsampa • Barley flour mixed with tea. It forms the staple diet of the Lo-pas, and is also used as a religious offering.

tulku • The recognized incarnation of a deceased high lama.

Photographer...................... Vanessa Schuurbeque Boeye

Author.............................. Clara Marullo

Art/Design Director........... Dana Jinkins

Editorial Director.............. Jill Bobrow

Editor............................... Tara Hamilton

Production Assistant.......... Bonnie Atwater

Design Assistant................. Randi Jinkins

Project Development......... Gary Chassman

Map created by................... Howard Moses

Map production.................. Brooke Cunningham

Additional Photographs..... Tony Miller